Odd and Even

by Marilyn Deen

DISCARD

Consultant:
Adria F. Klein, PhD
California State University, San Bernardino

CAPSTONE PRESS
a capstone imprint

Wonder Readers are published by Capstone Press,
1710 Roe Crest Drive, North Mankato, Minnesota 56003.
www.capstonepub.com

Library of Congress Cataloging-in-Publication Data
Deen, Marilyn.
  Odd and even / Marilyn Deen—1st ed.
    p. cm.—(Wonder readers)
  Includes index.
  ISBN 978-1-4296-9608-1 (library binding)
  ISBN 978-1-4296-7933-6 (paperback)
  ISBN 978-1-62065-366-1 (ebook PDF)
  1. Numbers, Natural—Juvenile literature. I. Title.
  QA141.3.D44 2013
  513—dc23   2011022023

Summary: Simple text and color photographs describe the difference between odd and even numbers,
how to skip-count using odds and evens, and what happens when you add them together.

Note to Parents and Teachers

The Wonder Readers: Mathematics series supports national mathematics standards. These titles use text structures that support early readers, specifically with a close photo/text match and glossary. Each book is perfectly leveled to support the reader at the right reading level, and the topics are of high interest. Early readers will gain success when they are presented with a book that is of interest to them and is written at the appropriate level.

Printed in the United States of America in North Mankato, Minnesota.
042012   006682CGF12

Table of Contents

Odd or Even?

This picture shows 1 kitten. 1 is an odd number. Other odd numbers are 3, 5, 7, 9, and 11.

This picture shows 2 dogs. 2 is an even number. Other even numbers are 4, 6, 8, 10, and 12.

There are 3 dogs in this picture. The only way to separate these dogs into 2 groups is to have 2 dogs in one group and 1 dog in the other group. Those groups are not the same. That is because 3 is an odd number.

There are 4 kittens in this picture.
You can separate them into
2 equal groups by having 2 kittens
in each group. That is because
4 is an even number.

1 2 3 4 5 6 7 8 9

Count these candles from 1 to 9.
Even numbers are always **between**
odd numbers. Odd numbers are
always between even numbers.

Only the even numbers are shown below. The odd numbers are missing. See if you can say the names of the missing odd numbers.

Skip-Counting

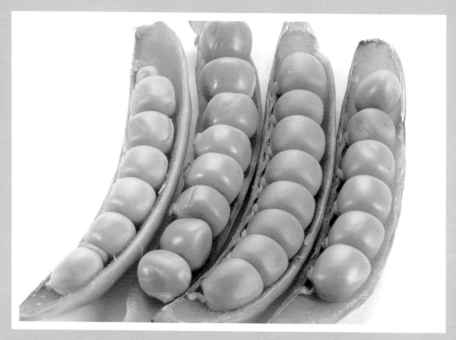

There are lots of peas on this page. See if you can **skip-count** only the odd-**numbered** peas. Start at 1 and end at 9.

Now finish skip-counting the peas, beginning with 11 and ending at 21. Then see how much higher you can count using only odd numbers, beginning with 21.

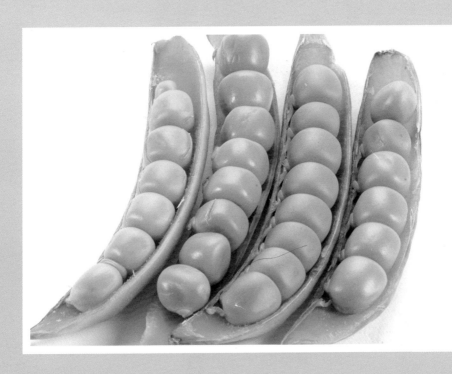

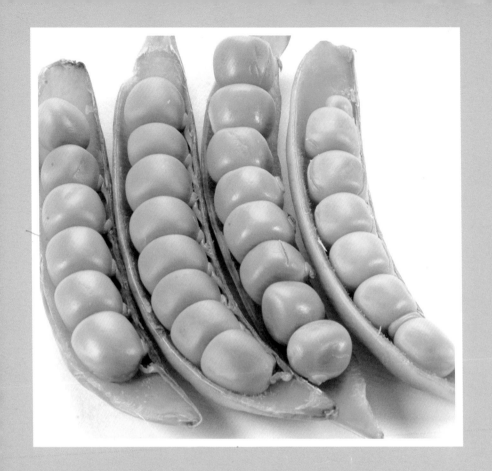

Now try to skip-count just the even-numbered peas. Start at 0 and end at 14.

See if you can skip-count the even-numbered peas from 16 to 28. Then see how much higher you can count using only even numbers.

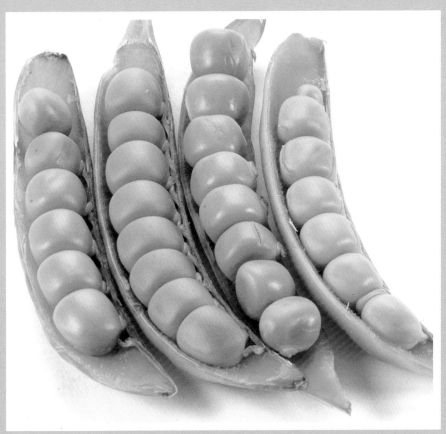

Odds Plus Evens

1 and 3 are both odd numbers. Add them together, and they make 4.
4 is an even number. Adding two odd numbers together will always make an even number.

2 and 4 are both even numbers. Add them together and they make 6. 6 is an even number. Adding two even numbers together will always make an even number.

1 is an odd number. 4 is an even number. Add them together and they make 5. The number 5 is an odd number. Adding an odd number and an even number together will always make an odd number.

Every number you can think of is either odd or even. Count this group of kids and decide if there is an odd or even number. Now look around and find other odd and even numbers. They're everywhere!

Glossary

between   having something on either side

numbered   having a number assigned

skip-count   to count by "jumping over" and leaving out some numbers

Now Try This!

Look for examples of odd-numbered and even-numbered items in your classroom. How many desks are there? Students? Days on the calendar? Windows? Then practice adding them together (chairs + desks). Discuss the answers you get with your friends.

Internet Sites

FactHound offers a safe, fun way to find Internet sites related to this book. All of the sites on FactHound have been researched by our staff.

Here's all you do:

Visit *www.facthound.com*

Type in this code: 9781429696081

 **Super-cool stuff!** Check out projects, games and lots more at **www.capstonekids.com**

Index

Editorial Credits

Maryellen Gregoire, project director; Mary Lindeen, consulting editor; Gene Bentdahl, designer;
    Sarah Schuette, editor; Wanda Winch, media researcher; Eric Manske, production specialist

Photo Credits

All images by Capstone Studio: Karon Dubke

Word Count: **388**   Guided Reading Level: **J**   Early Intervention Level: **18**